For

The Older I Get The Better I Am

Edited by
Lois L. Kaufman and Claudine Gandolfi

Illustrations by Murray Callahan

Design by Arlene Greco

PETER PAUPER PRESS, INC.
WHITE PLAINS, NEW YORK

Text copyright © 1996
Peter Pauper Press, Inc.
202 Mamaroneck Avenue
White Plains, NY 10601
Illustrations copyright © 1996
Murray Callahan
All rights reserved
ISBN 0-88088-455-X
Printed in Singapore
7 6 5 4 3

Introduction

Everyone believes it, but Bernard Baruch
said it:

*To me, old age is always fifteen years older
than I am.*

Research shows that most of us agree that age
is really just a state of mind. Reaching age 60
set Gloria Steinem free. Lynn Redgrave feels
that getting used to her age led her to accept
herself, and Doris Lessing finds that middle
age gives one the freedom of anonymity.

Let's keep active, physically and mentally. As
Frank Lloyd Wright put it, we should grow up
without getting old. Patti LaBelle wants to be
rockin' and rollin' at 105, and Helena
Rubinstein says a woman shouldn't tell the
truth about her age until she's over ninety.
Maybe not even then!

L. L. K.

I basically avoid anything I've done in the past. I'm living *now*.

Lynda Carter

I guess at my age I should feel a little older, but I don't . . . My body still feels like it wants to run in the park.

Lena Horne,
at age 67

That's the good thing about getting older: the experience. The problem is I keep forgetting what the experience was.

Bill Cosby

Memory is the diary that chronicles things that never have happened and couldn't possibly have happened.

Oscar Wilde

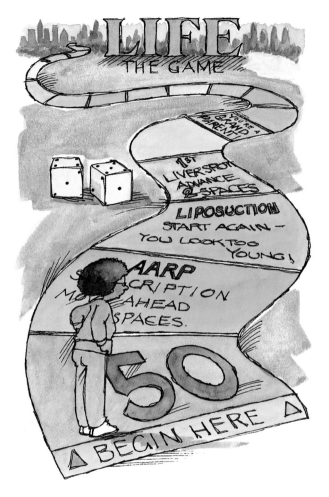

Some say that life begins at 50. So do liposuction, liver spots, thinning hair, and high fiber diets.

A woman is as old as she looks to a man who likes to look at her.

Finley Peter Dunne

Demographics are with us. There are more people over 55, and the discretionary dollar is there. The definition of old is beginning to move along. After all, America is only now beginning to admit that it is aging, after some 200-odd years.

Carmen,
model, at age 64

I'm in a very enviable position, being able to work like this forty-five years later. It's always beginning! I never have a sense of finishing up, just new things beginning. When I die, they're going to carry me off a stage.

Angela Lansbury

At 60 the fun doesn't end; there are just
more naps in between.

Women have been increasing their mental health and well-being over each generation, and now the majority in their 50s feel the greatest well-being of any stage in their lives.

Gail Sheehy

I might be an antique like the Stones, but antiques are valuable.

Billy Joel

One thing is certain, and I have always known it—the joys of my life have nothing to do with age.

May Sarton

Age to me means nothing. I can't get old; I'm working. I was old when I was twenty-one and out of work. As long as you're working, you stay young. When I'm in front of an audience, all that love and vitality sweeps over me and I forget my age.

George Burns

The best way to get some people to do
something is to suggest that they're too
old to do it.

The only thing about my life is the length of it. If I had to live my life again, I'd make all the same mistakes, only sooner.

Tallulah Bankhead

Being young is beautiful, but being old is comfortable.

Marie von Ebner-Eschenbach

I love every thing that's old; old friends, old times, old manners, old books, old wines.

Oliver Goldsmith

Look at a day when you are supremely satisfied at the end. It's not a day when you lounge around doing nothing; it's when you've had everything to do, and you've done it.

Margaret Thatcher

Old men forget. . . .
But he'll remember with advantages
What feats he did. . . .

William Shakespeare,
Henry V

To me, fair friend, you never can be old,
For as you were when first your eye I ey'd,
Such seems your beauty still.

William Shakespeare,
Sonnet

It's exciting to get old, with a body that still functions, though these days my spirit is doing most of the work. The early and middle experiences of your life take on a greater reality with age, and you gain an overview.

Barbara Morgan,
at age 83

What is real wisdom? It comes from life experience, well digested. It's not what comes from reading great books. When it comes to understanding life, experiential learning is the only worthwhile kind; everything else is hearsay.

Joan Erikson

At 50, sex isn't the 4th of July any more—
it's more like Thanksgiving!

In youth we believe many things that are not true; in old age we doubt many truths.

German Proverb

We arrive complete novices at the different ages of life, and we often want experience in spite of our years.

La Rochefoucauld

What though youth gave love and roses,
Age still leaves us friends and wine.

Thomas Moore

It gives me great pleasure to converse with the aged. They have been over the road that all of us must travel, and know where it is rough and difficult and where it is level and easy.

Plato

The older I get the more difficult it becomes for me to think of myself as old. In fact, the older I get the more difficult it becomes for me to think, period.

Youth, large, lusty, loving—youth full
    of grace, force, fascination,
Do you know that Old Age may come after
    you with equal grace, force, fascination?
                                    Walt Whitman

People's expectations of age have changed
a great deal. . . . There's a certain inner flex-
ibility. People no longer feel that at 50 it's
all over.
                                    Alice Adams

At twenty years of age, the will reigns; at
thirty, the wit; and at forty, the judgment.
                                    Benjamin Franklin

To be seventy years young is sometimes far
more cheerful and hopeful than to be forty
years old.
                                    Oliver Wendell Holmes

Isn't it nice to know that the older you get the more your childhood playthings are worth.

A man grows better humored as he grows older.

Samuel Johnson

Age and treachery will overcome youth and skill.

Anonymous

It is objected . . . that he is 77 years of age [too old for public office]; but at a much more advanced age, our Franklin was the ornament of human nature. He may not be able to perform, in person, all the details of his office; but if he gives us the benefit of his understanding, his integrity, his watchfulness, and takes care that all the details are well performed by himself or his necessary assistants, all public purposes will be answered.

Thomas Jefferson

As you get older your brain seems to gain the talents of a screen editor. Most of your memories are of good times and what you can't remember was best forgotten to begin with.

No man is ever so old but he thinks he can live another year.

Cicero

Women sit, or move to and fro—
    some old some young;
The young are beautiful—but the old
    are more beautiful than the young.

Walt Whitman

We grow with years more fragile in body, but morally stouter, and we can throw off the chill of a bad conscience almost at once.

Logan Pearsall Smith

Please don't retouch my wrinkles; it took me so long to earn them.

Anna Magnani,
who didn't want the studio stills for
The Rose Tattoo airbrushed

An old log burns brighter than a green twig.

The old know what they want; the young are sad and bewildered.

Logan Pearsall Smith

So long as a man still has inspiration and the will to go on, he still exemplifies youth.

Maurice J. Lewi

Give me a young man in whom there is something of the old, and an old man with something of the young: guided so, a man may grow old in body, but never in mind.

Cicero

Questioned about when I should retire, I said, "I'm going to fight to pass a bill that would force a mandatory retirement age on boxers—sixty-five."

George Foreman,
By George

A woman should maintain a certain sense
of mystery about herself, and I think that
can continue to any age.

Angela Lansbury

Many a man that couldn't direct ye to th'
drug store on th' corner when he was thirty
will get a respectful hearin' when age has
further impaired his mind.

Finley Peter Dunne

Lots of old people don't get wise, but you
don't get wise unless you age.

Joan Erikson

You become more of yourself, a truth-teller.
You don't care that much what other people think. Sure, you've made mistakes, you
have some pains, but you become more and
more whole . . . you're not driven by things
like you were when you were younger. You
can take risks in new ways. It's a subtle
thing. You can show more of the reality of
yourself instead of hiding behind a mask
for fear of revealing too much.

Betty Friedan,
on aging

The calendar is not your worst enemy. It's
the gravity that gets you in the end.

As an actor you can work into your 50s and longer. A lot of actors do their best work when they're older.

Dolph Lundgren

I feel a little . . . bit of what it must be like to be a Miss World or Miss Universe. And it happening [in] my 52nd year was as unexpected as it could possibly be.

Patrick Stewart

I'm enjoying getting older. Older faces are more interesting—particularly my face, which was a little on the bland side when I was younger.

Christopher Reeve

So many candles, so little cake.

Surely the consolation prize of age is in finding out how few things are worth worrying over, and how many things that we once desired, we don't want anymore.

Dorothy Dix

Let's face it: mandatory retirement is a terrible idea. I've always felt it was ridiculous that when a guy reaches sixty-five, no matter what shape he's in, we retire him instantly. We should be depending on our older executives. They have the experience. They have the wisdom.

Lee Iacocca

It would have been comforting to know at age 21 that by the age of 39, or so, I would have the confidence to do and say what I thought was right without scorn or ridicule. Getting older is not so bad, after all.

Sandra Day O'Connor,
quoted by Diane Sawyer

Remember when you thought "Middle Age
Spread" was a sandwich filling for the
over-50 crowd?

Youth is a circumstance you can't do anything about. The trick is to grow up without getting old.

Frank Lloyd Wright

I have enjoyed greatly the second blooming that comes when you finish the life of the emotions and of personal relations; and suddenly find—at the age of fifty, say—that a whole new life has opened before you, filled with things you can think about, study, or read about. . . . It is as if a fresh sap of ideas and thoughts was rising in you.

Agatha Christie

In youth we learn; in age we understand.

Marie von Ebner-Eschenbach

Looks fade but wit endures.

Evelyn Loeb

Life is like riding a bicycle; you don't fall off
unless you stop pedaling.

Claude Pepper

It's easier to quit smoking as you get older. Although older smokers' habits are stronger because they've been at it longer, they've also had more experience at trying to quit cigarettes—and statistics show that in this area, practice helps to make perfect.

William Schones

Alonso of Aragon was wont to say in commendation of age, that age appears to be best in four things—old wood best to burn, old wine to drink, old friends to trust, and old authors to read.

Francis Bacon

Years may wrinkle the skin, but to give up interest wrinkles the soul.

Douglas MacArthur

Advise those old fellows of ours to follow my
example; keep up your spirits, and that will
keep up your bodies; you will no more stoop
under the weight of age than if you had swal-
lowed a handspike.

Benjamin Franklin

Man reaches the highest point of lovable-
ness at 12 to 17—to get it back, in a second
flowering, at the age of 70 to 90.

Isak Dinesen

Your mind expands as your body shrinks,
and you adjust to it, giving in age what you
couldn't give in youth.

Laurence Olivier

I wish I had a penny for every post-
menopausal wild girl who's told me she's
off to track gorillas in the Congo without
her husband, or she's setting off with
another woman friend to climb mountains,
or she's resuscitated her tennis game and is
now entering tournaments.

Gail Sheehy

To me, old age is always fifteen years older
than I am.

Bernard Baruch

You think you've got it rough now? In the old days we used a stone tablet and chisel as a memo pad.

I'm not worried about getting older because I'm getting better. I can hold a note longer. I can sing a song better. At 50, you know a lot about yourself and I feel I can teach people important things about getting to this stage in life . . . Hopefully, you'll see me rockin' and rollin' at 105!

Patti LaBelle

To indulge in one's emotions is a privilege allowed to the elderly.

Cary Grant,
crying at being named Man of the Year, 1982

Don't pick on me because I'm old. I have too many other qualities to make fun of!

Anonymous

When you look the way I do, why not brag.

June Lockhart,
at 70

When men reach their sixties and retire
they go to pieces. Women just go right on
cooking.

Gail Sheehy

Middle age may be a time of increased health. People ages 45 to 64 spend fewer days away from their jobs fighting an illness than do people ages 15 to 44. And in a recent study of 435,000 adults, older people reported more "good health days" per month than younger people.

Jill Grigsby, Ph.D.

I just did a gig at Treasure Island Casino. I didn't have groupies, I had AARPies [American Association of Retired Persons]. They don't throw panties onstage . . . they give you a good mutual fund or a mustard plaster.

Pat Harrington

So much has been said and sung of beautiful young girls, why doesn't somebody wake up to the beauty of old women?

Harriet Beecher Stowe,
Uncle Tom's Cabin

If we could sell our experiences for what
they cost us we'd be millionaires.

Abigail Van Buren

Our sense of humor improves as we get older, partly because we stop "editing" ourselves to avoid negative reactions as we did in earlier years. Since some researchers believe that laughter helps heal the body and keep it well, it's great to know that "the best medicine" is in ample and growing supply throughout old age.

Steve Allen, Jr., M.D.

My memory is very good: I can make the same mistakes today that I made 50 years ago.

Simon Rothschild

The frightening thing about middle age is knowing you'll grow out of it.

Doris Day

Middle age is that time in a man's life
when his daydreams center around a
banker's saying yes instead of a girl.

Jane Fonda

In your amours you should prefer old Women to young ones . . . because they have more knowledge of the world and their Minds are better stored with Observations; their Conversation is more improving, and more lastingly agreeable. . . .

Benjamin Franklin

When researchers did a study of 59 women runners age 40 or over, they found that women in their fifties had better body-image than women in their forties. That positive image is something anyone can achieve at any age.

Wendy Kohrt, Ph.D.

Getting older means I'm no longer in the service industry.

Gloria Goldstein,
mother of 3 grown children

Here's to another year, and let's hope it's
above ground.

Carol Shields,
The Stone Diaries

You put such a stress on passion when you're young. You learn about the value of tenderness when you grow old. You also learn in late life not to hold, to give without hanging on; to love freely, in the sense of wanting nothing in return.

Joan Erikson

A man is not old as long as he is seeking something.

Jean Rostand

Age . . . is a matter of feeling, not of years.

George William Curtis

If wrinkles must be written upon our brows, let them not be written upon the heart. The spirit should never grow old.

James A. Garfield

Middle age—when type gets small and your arms get short.

I don't deserve this, but then, I have arthritis and I don't deserve that, either.

Jack Benny,
on being given an award

One keeps forgetting old age up to the very brink of the grave.

Colette

I believe the true function of age is memory. I'm recording as fast as I can.

Rita Mae Brown

One should never make one's *début* with a scandal. One should reserve that to give an interest to one's old age.

Oscar Wilde

A new broom sweeps clean but the old one
knows the corners.

Proverb

Every now and then somebody asks me when I'm going to retire. *Retire?* . . . I will always be leading the cheers for life, and I hope that's the way people will always see me and remember me, as a cheerleader for life, out there in front of the crowd with a megaphone in my hand, crying out, "Gimme an L! Gimme an I! Gimme an F! Gimme an E! LIFE! LIFE! LIFE!

Mickey Rooney

I have discovered the secret formula for a carefree Old Age: ICR–FI–"If You Can't Recall It, Forget It."

Goodman Ace

My trick for looking and feeling young is being constantly on the go, meeting new people, seeing new things.

Diane Von Furstenberg

I don't feel eighty. In fact I don't feel *anything*
till noon. Then it's time for my nap.

Bob Hope

People get happier as they get older. A big chunk of that happiness comes from passing the decision-making hurdles of youth, such as whether you should marry, have kids, take that job or buy a new house. Now you're reaping the rewards of whatever decisions you made in the past.

Walter S. Smitson, Ph.D.

At twenty-one or twenty-two, so many things appear solid, permanent, and terrible, which forty sees as nothing but disappearing miasma. Forty can't tell twenty about this. Twenty can find out only by getting to be forty.

Joseph Cotten,
written in a letter in the movie,
The Magnificent Ambersons

The young sow wild oats. The old grow sage.

Winston Churchill

Time is a dressmaker specializing in alterations.
Faith Baldwin

Turning 60 is more like a beginning. I'm free. I can take chances. . . . It used to take two years of wild passion before I became friends with a lover. Now, it's immediate. A part of my brain is free.

Gloria Steinem

Over the last few years, my comfort level with how I look has improved. My age has helped, you know. You get used to yourself and accept yourself.

Lynn Redgrave

I grow old ever learning many things.

Solon

It just takes that one person, an older someone who has lived life and seen things and made his way, to set you right. Then you can know yourself what's important and what to do.

Greta Garbo

"You're not getting older, you're getting better," says Dr. Joyce Brothers. This, however, is the kind of doctor who inspires a second opinion.

Bill Cosby

We turn not older with years, but newer every day.

Emily Dickinson

I think I exploded the myth that rock and roll is just for young people

Paul McCartney,
at age 47, about a sold-out concert

Youth is a disease from which we all recover.

Dorothy Fuldheim

Compared to younger populations, twice as many older people say they find their sexual partner attractive.

Mark H. Beers, M.D.

When you look in the mirror and your mother
looks back you realize how beautiful she was.

I have always felt that a woman has the right to treat the subject of her age with ambiguity until, perhaps, she passes into the realm of over ninety. Then it is better she be candid with herself and with the world.

Helena Rubinstein

Being seventy is not a sin.

Golda Meir

I'll never make the mistake of being seventy again.

Casey Stengel

Time and trouble will tame an advanced young woman, but an advanced old woman is uncontrollable by any earthly force.

Dorothy L. Sayers

One boon to the middle years is that the clothes you've held on to finally come back into style—sort of.

All one's life as a young woman one is on show, a focus of attention, people notice you. You set yourself up to be noticed and admired. And then, not expecting it, you become middle-aged and anonymous. No one notices you. You achieve a wonderful freedom. It is a positive thing. You can move about, unnoticed and invisible.

Doris Lessing

'Tis a maxim with me to be young as long as one can: there is nothing can pay one for that invaluable ignorance which is the companion of youth; those sanguine groundless hopes, and that lively vanity, which make all the happiness of life. To my extreme mortification I grow wiser every day.

Lady Mary Wortley Montagu

The love we have in our youth is superficial compared to the love that an old man has for his old wife.

Will Durant,
on his 90th birthday

By middle age one has witnessed many
technological advances, but none so
wonderful as the elastic waistband.

No Spring, nor Summer beauty hath
    such grace,
As I have seen in one Autumnal face.

John Donne

The young man knows the rules but the old
man knows the exceptions.

Oliver Wendell Holmes

I'm at the age where I've got to prove that
I'm just as good as I never was.

Rex Harrison

Though it sounds absurd, it is true to say I
felt younger at sixty than I had felt at twenty.

Ellen Glasgow

Phyllis Diller once said, in comparing herself to a beauty queen, "We take the same
bra size, only she takes a regular and I
take a long."

I never feel age. . . . If you have creative work, you don't have age or time.

Louise Nevelson

The secret to brandy is age. The secret to everything is age.

Anthony Quinn,
spoken in the movie
A Walk in the Clouds

The older the violin the sweeter the music.

Anonymous

A joy ride now means having my back support in the car.

Bumper sticker on large luxury RV: We're
out spending our children's inheritance.

It doesn't bother me.

Cary Grant,
to his mother,
who criticized his graying hair

Maybe not, but it bothers me. It makes me seem so old.

Cary Grant's mother,
then in her nineties

To get back one's youth, one has merely to repeat one's follies.

Oscar Wilde

No age or time of life, no position or circumstance, has a monopoly on success. Any age is the right age to *start doing!*

Gerard